HOW TO HELP
A GUIDE TO
Giving
Back

WAYS TO HELP
THE
ELDERLY

Tamra Orr

Mitchell Lane
PUBLISHERS

P.O. Box 196
Hockessin, DE 19707
www.mitchelllane.com

Mitchell Lane
PUBLISHERS

HOW TO HELP
A GUIDE TO
Giving
Back

Ways to Help After a Natural Disaster
Ways to Help Children With Disabilities
Ways to Help Chronically Ill Children
Ways to Help Disadvantaged Youth
Ways to Help in Your Community
Ways to Help the Elderly
Volunteering in Your School
Celebrities Giving Back

Library of Congress
Cataloging-in-Publication Data

Orr, Tamra.
  Ways to help the elderly / by Tamra Orr.
      p. cm. — (How to help : a guide to giving
back)
  Includes bibliographical references and
index.
  ISBN 978-1-58415-915-5 (library bound)
  1. Older people—Care—Juvenile literature.
2. Older people—Juvenile literature. 3.
Helping behavior—Juvenile literature. 4.
Children—Conduct of life—Juvenile literature.
I. Title.
  HQ1061.O77 2011
  305.26—dc22
                                                    2010006539

Printing   1   2   3   4   5   6   7   8   9

                                                    PLB

CONTENTS

Introduction

Holding on to memories is not always simple. They slip away too easily. How well can you remember what you did last month? Last year? Five years ago? If you're in your 70s, 80s, or 90s, remembering the past is even harder. Memories fade as the years pass, and important names and special moments are often lost. One group of school students decided to help some of the older adults in their community hold on to those precious memories a whole lot longer.

Kayla Baldwin, a student from the Key Learning Community in the Indianapolis public school system, was volunteering at a local church's day program for senior citizens when she came up with an idea to help honor and hold the stories of these people's lives.

Baldwin and ten other students began spending their afternoons sitting with the elderly and interviewing them about their lives. They asked about time spent in the military or trips taken to other parts of the world. They asked about children's names and favorite events. Then, armed with scissors, construction paper, and glue, they began creating scrapbooks of each person's life. Adding photographs to

their borders, they slowly gathered memories and put them between covers. When the scrapbooks were finished, the members of the program gathered to share them and tell stories. "It's wonderful," says Susan Dinnin, the program director. "The kids just have a way of energizing our people and forging relationships. It's great for them both."[1]

Like Kayla and her friends, one way to give back to your community is to help the people who were part of it long before you came along. The elderly often struggle with many tasks, from daily routine activities such as grocery shopping or taking out the trash to dealing with periods of loneliness or depression. You can make a real difference by taking the time to lend a hand or just an ear. Your parents or other adults in your life can help you find a way to volunteer. Whether you help by doing some housework, reading a book out loud, writing a card, or just sharing your time, you can change someone's life and make his or her world a better place.

1. "Students Make Scrapbooks out of Seniors' Lives," The Indianapolis Star, December 21, 2009.

A young boy eats a meal in a café with an elderly woman. Taking time to talk to someone older than you is not only fun for both of you, but it can teach you important lessons about life. What questions might you ask? What could you learn?

Chapter 1

Dinnertime!

You can become a volunteer at Meals on Wheels.

Can you imagine being hungry and not being able to leave the house to go to the grocery store, pull out a snack from the refrigerator or cupboard, or stop by your favorite fast-food restaurant for a quick bite? For more than five million senior citizens in the United States, this is exactly what happens. They are not able to get to the next hot meal because they don't have transportation, they are in poor health, or they are not able to afford enough groceries. Can you change that? Yes, you can!

Long ago, during World War II, German planes dropped bombs on the people of England. Many of the English lost their homes—and, in the process, their kitchens and food supplies. Families were suddenly desperate and hungry. A group of women volunteers got together to help take care of this emergency. They prepared and brought meals to their neighbors. They took water and food to the soldiers out on the battlefield. They soon earned the nickname of Meals on Wheels.

Spending time in the kitchen together can help make meal time more interesting, plus the two of you might discover some new recipes.

After the war, the tradition to help others in need continued. In 1954, the first home-delivered meal program was started in Philadelphia, Pennsylvania. It was followed by another program in Columbus, Ohio. Since then, it has spread throughout the entire country. Today, Meals on Wheels prepares and delivers meals to homebound seniors in local communities throughout the United States.[1]

How can you help make sure that the elderly in your neighborhood are not hungry? Along with your school, church, or family, you can become a volunteer at Meals on Wheels. There are a number of ways you can assist. You might be part of the team that prepares the meals. You might pack them into boxes and load them into the back of vans, trucks, or cars. You could be one of the people who ride from door to door to deliver the hot food. Perhaps you will be the volunteer known as the runner, who rings the front doorbell and greets seniors with a friendly hello. Imagine how happy you could make each person when you arrive with hot food and a warm smile.

Another way you can help Meals on Wheels is through helping at events and fund-raisers the organization hosts. Perhaps you will help put up decorations or fill out name tags. You could make phone calls or organize lists. Maybe you can just lend a hand in the office or the kitchen. No matter what role you take on, you can know that you are helping the elderly in your community go to bed with a full stomach, and a fuller heart.

1. Meals on Wheels Association of America, http://www.mowaa.org.

Chapter **2**

Time for a Visit

One way to help is by reading a newspaper or book to an elderly person who cannot see well.

Have you ever looked up to see that a favorite friend or relative has stopped by for a visit? It is a great feeling. You get the chance to spend time with someone you really like and whose company you enjoy.

For the many millions of elderly people who are living alone, a visit can mean even more. It means a new face, interesting news, good conversation, and contact with the outside world. It means that someone cares and wants to pass the time with them—a feeling that people of any age can appreciate.

How can you find a person to visit? Talk to your parents or teachers. They can help you check with local hospitals, assisted living residences, and nursing homes. They might also be able to guide you to relatives or neighbors who could benefit from regular visits from you. You can visit people with a group or organization, a family member, or another adult.

Once you know whom to visit, you might wonder what to do once you are there. After all, a visit is not much fun for anyone if you just sit there checking your watch. There are

Just as you can spend time reading aloud to an older adult, he or she might also help you understand your homework or explain something you are working on at school.

ways to avoid this. For example, before you stop by, make a list of topics to talk about when you arrive. You can ask about their lives—their past, their children, and their interests. You can also tell them about what is happening in your life. What are you studying in school? What did you and your friends do over the weekend? Tell them about your brothers and sisters, your pets, or your parents. Talk about things that are going on in the world and in the national and local headlines. Some of these topics will interest the people you visit—some will not. Pay attention so you will know which topics to focus on and which to avoid the next time you stop by.

Along with just talking, another helpful service you can offer is reading out loud. Many senior citizens cannot see well enough to read anymore. Reading newspaper stories, magazine articles, personal letters, and favorite books can be wonderful to do for someone.

If you do read aloud to someone, keep a few things in mind. First, read slowly—much more so than you would normally. Second, read louder than usual. Third, put emotion into what you read—make it interesting. You don't want to speak in a boring monotone. Vary your pace and style. Finally, when reading aloud, be patient. Be willing to repeat things or read something that might not be personally interesting to you. Remember, no matter what you are doing while you are there, you are actually giving someone a gift of your time. Whether you just sit and chat or you read the next two chapters of an old classic novel, you are sharing a part of yourself with someone who needs it.

Chapter **3**

Bring a Friend

Nearly everyone loves pets, even the elderly.

Visiting an elderly person in his or her home or at an assisted living residence is a wonderful thing to do—but how can you make your trip more interesting? Bring along your pet.

Studies have shown that a friendly dog can help ease an elderly person's loneliness. It also helps them feel happier! In fact, it works so well, it does not even have to be a real dog. In a study done by Saint Louis University, people in three different nursing homes were given the chance to spend time with a cute little dog named Sparky or a silver, metal robot dog named Aibo. After seven weeks, the residents all answered questions about how lonely they felt. Those who had spent time with the pups—real or robotic—were happier overall.[1]

Next time you plan a visit, consider bringing along your pet. The person you are spending time with may be as excited to see it as he or she is to see you. Petting an animal

1. Saint Louis University. "Doggie Robot Eases Loneliness in Nursing Home Residents as Well as Real Dog, Study Finds." *ScienceDaily,* February 26, 2008. http://www. sciencedaily.com /releases/2008/02/080225213636.htm.

 Being around a dog or cat can help an older person feel happier and healthier. Taking your pet for a walk with the person can also help him or her get some fresh air and exercise.

often helps a person feel less alone. It is also relaxing. Scientific studies have shown that stroking a dog's or cat's fur, for example, lowers a person's blood pressure and heart rate. It is soothing to the animal—and to the human! Animals often remind the elderly of pets they had in the past and inspire stories to relate and share. One veterinarian stated, "In cases where animals are used in nursing homes, it's absolutely spectacular the way [they] can turn people around. A withdrawn person comes out of his shell."[2]

What kind of pet can you bring with you? It depends. If you are going to visit a person's home, be sure to ask first if he or she has any allergies to animals or are frightened by them. If you are going into a nursing home or assisted living residence, on the other hand, call first and ask if pets are permitted. Ask if there are any special rules about them, too. Never bring in an animal without permission.

Dogs are often the best choice, as long as they are well behaved, follow commands, like strangers, and never bite! They should also be kept on a leash at all times, and if they make a mess, you have to be ready to clean it up immediately. Bringing along a bowl for water and a snack is also a good idea.

Do other pets work? They might. Cats can come, but it is harder to keep track of them. While pets like birds, turtles, guinea pigs, or hamsters might also be permitted, they are not quite as cuddly and easy to pet.

Visits from someone who cares are wonderful. Visits that include a tail-wagging dog or a purring cat can be even better.

---

2. Sharon L. Bass. "Nursing-Home Pets a Boon to Residents." *The New York Times,* http://www.nytimes.com/1986/06/01/nyregion/nursing-home-pets-a-boon-to-residents.html?&pagewanted=1

Chapter 4

Through the Seasons

Temperature changes can affect the elderly, so make sure they have proper heat for winter and air-conditioning or fans for summer.

Look out the window. Is the sidewalk covered in leaves? Is it exceptionally windy? Is there snow on the ground? Is the thermometer soaring up into the triple digits or dropping to single ones? If so, you have an opportunity to help!

Elderly people who live alone or with an elderly spouse may not be able to get out of the house and do what they want to because Mother Nature is making it too difficult. They may also be struggling to cope with extreme temperatures. When you are older, it is harder to adapt to temperature highs and lows. This is where your hard work can make a huge difference.

Spring is often an easy season, but it can bring strong winds. If you know an elderly person nearby, talk to your parents and make a plan to stop in. You can help make sure shutters are strong and tree limbs haven't fallen. In the summer, keep an eye on the temperature. If it starts getting hot, stop by to see if the older people have fans or if air conditioners are working. Encourage them to drink a lot of water and stay indoors during the worst of the weather. You

During a heat wave in Minneapolis, Emily Strand, a member of Little Brothers—Friends of the Elderly, stopped by Verona Halvorson's apartment to put together a fan to help her keep cool.

and your parents might consider taking the elderly to an air-conditioned restaurant, store, or other cool location on the hottest days.

In the autumn, stop by and help clear off porches, sidewalks, and driveways of leaves. These leaves can be quite slippery following a rain shower.

Winter brings the most danger. Snow and ice on sidewalks, steps, and driveways can cause a life-threatening fall for an older person. Shoveling these areas to keep them clear, as

A breath of fresh air is often just what the elderly need. If possible, take a walk together. Even if it is raining, you might take a short stroll—just be sure to hold on to the umbrella.

well as putting down salt, can help lessen the risk. Extremely cold temperatures can also be a problem. Older people are vulnerable to hypothermia, or the accidental lowering of the core body temperature below 95°F. Stopping by to make sure the elderly stay inside, keep the heat on, and wear an extra sweater can make these chilly days easier to handle.

No matter what time of year it is, there is always something you can do to make the days brighter and safer for senior citizens. Just take a moment to stop by and see what needs to be done.

Chapter 5

Outside Time

Help an elderly person with outdoor chores such as mowing the lawn or shoveling snow.

You may have already noticed how many chores there are to do at your house, especially outside. In the spring and summer, grass keeps growing, so it needs to be mowed every week or so. Weeds have to be pulled, gardens watered, and bushes trimmed. Bird baths and bird feeders need to be refilled. In the fall, leaves pile up everywhere and need to be raked and sometimes bagged. There is always a lot to be done, and just when you think you are caught up, a new season brings new chores.

For the elderly, many of these outdoor chores are physically difficult and even dangerous for them to do. You can help them by taking over, with an adult's assistance. Find out what chores need to be done and then offer to do them on a regular basis. You will need to ask how much equipment the person already has and what you will need to bring with you (lawn mower, brooms, rakes, clippers, etc.). Of course, you will have to be extra careful with the equipment and follow all of the safety precautions.

 People who grew up planting backyard gardens may miss being able to put seeds and bulbs into the ground. Helping them garden can be a wonderful way to give them a smile—and happy memories.

Find ways to involve the elderly person as much as you can. Have them keep you company, and chat together, while you work. Spend time just talking before or after your chore is finished. Look through seed catalogs and fill out the order for them. Take out some paper and plot what the garden should look like. Sit and watch the birds taking a bath in fresh water or the squirrels sidle up to the bird feeder for a sneaky snack. Ask the senior citizens' advice and guidance on what you are doing. If they have a different way of trimming the bushes or a different method of planting seeds, listen to them and try to follow their directions. Ask questions! These older people have years of experience and wisdom, and you can learn from them if you take the time to pay attention and hear what they have to say.

When you have finished whatever chore you came to do, be sure to clean up after yourself. Don't leave a mess behind. Put all equipment away. Take sacks of leaves to the curb. Sweep up if you've been digging and there's dirt scattered around. Look over the work you've done and make sure you've made things better!

Before you leave, also make note of when you will need to come back and do it again since grass, plants, and weeds grow; leaves fall; and animals use up their food and water. You can be sure that everyone will eagerly anticipate your next visit.

Chapter **6**

Adopt a Grandfriend

The bond between young and old people can prove to be a rewarding experience.

Have you ever wished you had a bigger family? Have you ever wished your grandparents were still around or lived closer to you? You might find the solution to any of these situations by choosing to adopt a grandfriend.

The word *grandfriend,* according to Martin Kimeldorf, author of *The Grandfriends Project: A Program Creating Friendships across the Generations,* means "(1) a young and older person who befriend each other; (2) a person you know well or are fond of or (3) a volunteer or mentor to another generation."[1]

Adopting a grandfriend can be a family event, or something your class at school wants to do. If you are part of a Girl Scout or Boy Scout troop, Campfire, or other organization, you might want this to be your newest project. Typically it involves these steps:

1. Martin Kimeldorf. *The Grandfriends Project.* http://amby.com/kimeldorf/
intergenerational/GFP_01.html

1. Find an elderly person who needs some extra family. Ask your parents to help look for someone in the neighborhood or contact local nursing homes and ask who could use some visitors.

Irene Hendrickson blows out candles on her birthday cake as a visiting student watches. Students from Arizona Virtual Academy have "adopted" several senior citizens, including Hendrickson.

2. Go for a visit. Introduce yourself (along with others in your family). Ask questions and find out about the person. Kimeldorf writes, "Your grandfriends will look forward to your visits. . . . You are providing a very important service-friendship. . . . The exchange between young and old people and the sharing of stories across the generations can prove to be a very rewarding experience."[2]

3. Visit your grandfriends on a regular basis. In between visits, you can call them to say hello or even send an occasional card or letter. Let them know you are thinking about them.

If your new grandfriend is in a nursing home and you've never been to one before, it is important to keep a few things in mind. First of all, you should conduct yourself with respect for the people there. This is not the place for loud music, swearing, or other types of boisterous behavior. You should walk in with a good attitude; you are there to help.

Second, some of the people in the nursing home may be sick and need extra medical care and equipment. Some older people also have a condition called Alzheimer's disease. This illness makes it hard for them to remember things, and they may often be confused. Ask your teacher or parents about Alzheimer's so that you can understand how to communicate with someone who has this affliction. If being around people with illnesses or unfamiliar medical equipment makes you uncomfortable, ask questions and find out more about what is going on. Learning about unfamiliar things often makes them less mysterious and easier to accept.

2. Kimeldorf.

VOLUNTEER

Although older people may have some physical or mental illnesses, they can still be wonderful friends to spend time with.

You can volunteer for Shaping Lives, a program that pairs students with the residents of area senior care facilities. The group creates art projects based on children's books.

If you are still uncomfortable, talk to your parents and see if they can help.

Last, approach each visit like a chance to spend time with a friend. If you act like it is a chore, the elderly person will know and could be hurt. Adopting a grandfriend is a kind thing to do. As Kimeldorf adds, "Perhaps, someday far in the future, when you are much older . . . you'll yearn for a visitor. If you're lucky, another young adult—with a heart as big as yours—will come and be your grandfriend."[3]

3. Kimeldorf.

Chapter 7

Teaching Time

Teach older people new skills or new technology.

In school, you spend a great deal of time being taught new skills and information by your teachers. If you spend some time with an elderly person, however, you may find yourself in the opposite role. You may get to be the teacher for a change!

Teaching older people new skills is one way of helping them. Often they may feel left behind by today's changing technology. The idea of using a computer or sending a text message may be intimidating, or even frightening, for them. This can lead to their feeling less independent and more isolated from what is happening in the world.

With patience and time, you can help address these fears. Starting simply and slowly, you can explain how technology works, such as cell phones and text messages or computers and e-mails. You can show older people how to use these modern pieces of equipment. Keeping it basic is essential. If you give them too much information at once, it can be overwhelming. Take the time to also teach some of the jargon that goes with these actions too, like *surfing the*

Net, chat speak like *LOL,* or *instant messaging.* You might also show them how to take and send a picture with a cell phone.

What other technology can you share? Explain what online sites like Facebook and MySpace are. Help them look

 The games you play may be quite confusing to the older generation. Show them how they work. Who knows? You might inspire them to give it a try too!

Even though you most likely deal with computers every day, the technology may be quite intimidating to the elderly. Are you patient enough to show them how it works? Take your time!

online to locate their family or some of their friends. Let them listen to your MP3™ players and discuss how music is downloaded from the computer. Explain how the different television remotes work, and which buttons do what.

Always keep in mind, however, that older people can teach you a few things, too. Although they may seem old-fashioned to you, they may know some fantastic skills you've never learned before. Perhaps they can carve figures out of wood or knit a pair of socks. Maybe they can tell you what it is like to change the oil in your car or build a birdhouse. If you both take the time to share your knowledge, both of you will benefit!

Chapter **8**

Keep It Safe

Some elderly people cannot get around well, so you can help them with household chores.

There is a lot involved in taking care of an apartment or house—just ask your parents! Things need to be replaced and repaired all the time. This kind of maintenance is frequently hard to do for older people. They can't reach, they can't remember, or it is just too hard physically. With some help from an adult, a few tools, and a little training, you can take over a number of these simple jobs.

What are some jobs you can do to help out? For example, you can change the batteries in smoke alarms. It is quick and easy to do, and all you need is a ladder and the right batteries. Changing the air filter on a furnace is also simple and requires no tools.

Another possibility is replacing or repairing a doorknob or lock. It usually requires nothing more than a screwdriver. Fixing a loose nail takes only a hammer—and good aim. Replacing storm windows with screens on older houses is simple and fast. Cleaning the tracks of sliding glass doors is messy but makes it much easier to open and close them.

 Simple household chores like doing dishes can be difficult for some. Offer to lend a helping hand. Two can get things done much faster than one.

Bring a friend along to help you. You and your friend have the power to put a big smile on an elderly person's face.

How about washing and waxing someone's car? It is the perfect job for a hot summer day and makes a big difference in how a vehicle looks. Making sure the tires are properly inflated is also helpful.

When you stop by to visit, you might offer to do some regular household chores as well. Do the dishes. Clean out the refrigerator. Dust the highest shelves or do a load of laundry. Empty the trash and take out the garbage. Vacuum the carpets and sweep the kitchen floor. Change the sheets on the bed or replace the towels in the bathroom.

If you aren't sure where to start, ask what you can do to help, what needs a little fixing, or what needs to be replaced. Although your efforts may be easy and take only a few minutes, they will likely give the elderly person peace of mind and let him or her feel just a little safer and more secure.

Off on Errands

By helping the elderly take care of their regular errands, you will ensure that they have the things they need.

Have you ever gone along with your family when they run their usual errands? Perhaps they stop at the bank or the post office. They might make a trip to the grocery store or the pharmacy. The elderly frequently need these errands run as well but are unable to do them because of health problems or transportation issues. Perhaps, with some help from your parents or other adults, you can help take over some of these routine errands for them.

As always, one of the best places to start is by asking the person you are visiting what they need. Could you pick up some groceries for them each week? Do they need a prescription refilled? Perhaps you could pick up or drop off some library books, movies, or magazines. You might bring them some stamps or mail a package at the post office.

Other errands you might be able to do along with your parents include depositing checks at the bank, paying bills, picking up or dropping off movies, filling up the gas tank, stopping by the dry cleaner, taking the person to doctor's appointments, and walking pets.

Chapter 9

A bag of groceries, along with a visit from you, is often the best way to bring some happiness to an elderly person. Be sure to offer to help put the groceries away before you go!

Even though errands might not seem important, they are. They make sure you have what you need when you need it. By helping the elderly take care of their regular errands, you will ensure that they have the same thing.

Chapter 10

Happy Holidays

Share the holidays with an elderly person. Spread some kindness and cheer.

The holidays are a special time of year. They are often filled with family time, celebrations, and anticipation. For the elderly, however, the holidays can be one of the hardest times of the year. They may miss loved ones who are gone or live far away. They may long for days gone by. The holidays are a special time to reach out and help.

What can you do to help make Thanksgiving, Christmas or Hannukah, and New Year's a better time? Here are just a few suggestions.

Help the elderly write out their greeting cards. Ask them to whom they would like to send cards and what they would like to say, and then help them accomplish it. They can dictate messages and you can write them down. They might want to send letters to family or friends, so bring extra paper just in case. When you're done, address the envelopes, put on stamps, and make sure they all get to a mailbox.

Bring a special homemade treat or gift with you when you come to visit. This helps people know that you have

Decorating a Christmas tree should be done with the people you care about. During the holidays, help the elderly celebrate!

As with other holidays, birthdays are meant to be shared with family and friends—like you! Be prepared to help blow out candles—and sing!

been thinking of them and want to share your holiday traditions with them.

Check to see if any of the organizations, stores, or social services groups in your city are preparing food boxes. If they are, you can help with packaging, loading, or delivering them. You might also call your local food banks to see if they need help.

Why not take a holiday movie classic over to the your grandfriends' house and watch it with them? Ask them which one they like best, and stop by the movie rental store or check to see when it will be on television. You could also take over some music to share.

If the person you are visiting needs to pick up some gifts, you and your parents can offer to take them shopping. Or you can take a list and pick up whatever is needed. Bring over wrapping paper, tape, and labels and spend some time wrapping gifts together.

Although the people in nursing homes or assisted living residences are almost certain to have a special holiday meal, those who live alone may not have the chance. Talk to your parents about how you might share part of your meals with them. Maybe you could all stop by in the afternoon to share a plate of goodies, or even have the elderly person over to your house for dinner.

The holidays give you a special chance to share your time and spread some kindness. What better way to start off the new year than by making someone else's life a little happier?

NATIONAL RESOURCES

1-800-Volunteer.org
http://www.1-800-volunteer.org

AARP (American Association of Retired
    Persons)
601 E St. NW 4th Floor
Washington, D.C. 20049
202-434-6200
http://www.aarp.org/

Alzheimer's Association
225 N. Michigan Ave. 17th Floor
Chicago, IL 60601-7633
800-272-3900
http://www.alz.org/

Charity Vault
http://www.charity-charities.org/index.
    htm

Cross-Cultural Solutions
2 Clinton Place
New Rochelle, NY 10801
914-632-0022
http://www.crossculturalsolutions.org

Do Something.org
http://www.dosomething.org

Family Guide to Volunteering
Zoom into Action
http://www-tc.pbskids.org/zoom/
    grownups/action/pdfs/volunteer_
    guide.pdf

Feeding America
35 E. Wacker Drive. Suite 2000
Chicago, IL 60601
800-771-2303
http://feedingamerica.org/take-action/
    volunteer/volunteermatch.aspx

Idealist.org
http://www.idealist.org/

Junior Red Cross
Division of the American Red Cross
http://www.redcross.org

Learn and Serve America
The Corporation for National and
    Community Service
http://www.learnandserve.gov/

Little Brothers/Friends of the Elderly
National Headquarters
28 E. Jackson Blvd. Suite 405
Chicago, IL 60604-2357
312-786-1032
http://www.littlebrothers.org/

Meals on Wheels Association of America
203 S. Union St.
Alexandria, VA 22314
703-548-5558
http://www.mowaa.org/

National Council on Aging
1901 L St. NW 4th Floor
Washington, D.C. 20036
202-479-1200
http://www.ncoa.org/

National Holiday Project
321B Tennessee Avenue
Mill Valley, CA 94941
415-888-8243
http://www.holiday-project.org/

Network for Good
7920 Norfolk Ave. Suite 520
Bethesda, MS 20814
888-284-7978
http://www1.networkforgood.org/
    for-donors/volunteer

Serve.gov
The Corporation for National and
    Community Service
http://www.serve.gov/

USA Freedom Corps
http://www.volunteerkids.gov/

Volunteer Jobs
http://www.groovejob.com/

Volunteer Match
717 California St. Second Floor
San Francisco, CA 94108
415-241-6872
http://www.volunteermatch.org/

Volunteers of America
1660 Duke St.
Alexandria, VA 22314
703-341-5000
http://www.voa.org/

Youth Service America
http://www.ysa.org/

Youth Volunteer Corps of America
4600 W. 51st St. Suite 300
Shawnee Mission, KS 66205
913-432-3313
http://www.yvca.org/

Alabama
Montgomery Area Council on Aging
115 East Jefferson St.
Montgomery, AL 36104
334-263-0532
http://www.macoa.org/

Alaska
Calling Care.Com/Alaska
http://www.callingcare.com/care-
    providers-alaska.htm

Arizona
Duet: Partners in Health and Aging
555 West Glendale Avenue
Phoenix, AZ 85021
602-274-5022
http://www.centerdoar.org/

Handmaker
2221 N. Rosemont Blvd.
Tucson, AZ 85712
520-322-3622
http://www.handmaker.com/

Arkansas
Area Agency of Aging of Southeast
    Arkansas
709 East 8th Avenue
Pine Bluff, AR 71601
870-543-6300
http://www.aaasea.org/

RSVP of Central Arkansas
PO Box 5936
North Little Rock, AR 72119
501-604-4527
http://www.rsvpcenark.org/

California
Little Brothers/Friends of the Elderly
San Francisco Chapter
909 Hyde St. Room 628
San Francisco, CA 94109-4822
415-771-7957
http://sanfrancisco.littlebrothers.org/

National Senior Citizens Law Center
3435 Wilshire Blvd. Suite 2860
Los Angeles, CA 90010-1938
213-639-0930
and
1330 Broadway Suite 525
Oakland, CA 94612
510-663-1055
http://www.nsclc.org/

Wise and Healthy Aging
Ken Edwards Center
1527 4th St. Second Floor
Santa Monica, CA 90401
310-394-9871
http://www.wiseandhealthyaging.org/

Colorado
Seniors! Inc.
Denver Office
5840 E. Evans Ave.
Denver, CO 80222
303-300-6900
http://www.seniorsinc.org/

Connecticut
Connecticut Department of Elderly
    Services
10 Elmwood Place
Danbury, CT 06810
203-797-4686
http://www.ct.gov/agingservices/site/
    default.asp

Delaware

Delaware Association of Nonprofit
    Agencies
100 W. 10th St. Suite 102
Wilmington, DE 19801
302-777-5500
http://www.delawarenonprofit.org/

Volunteer Delaware
http://www.1-800-volunteer.org/1800Vol/
    volunteerdelaware/vcindex.do

Florida

Elder Care Services of Florida
2518 W. Tennessee St.
Tallahassee, FL 32304
850-921-5554
http://www.ecsbigbend.org/

Georgia

Volunteer! Decatur
PO Box 220
Decatur, GA 30031
678-553-6548
http://www.decaturga.com/cgs_
    citysvcs_ced_volunteer.aspx

Hawaii

Elderly Activities Division
127 Kamana St.
Hilo, HI 96720
808-961-8708
http://www.co.hawaii.hi.us/parks/ead/
    elderlyactivities.htm

Volunteer Hawaii
http://www.volunteerhawaii.org/index.
    php

Idaho

2-1-1 Idaho CareLine
1720 Westgate Dr., Suite A
Boise, ID 83704
208-332-7205
http://www.idahocareline.org/

Area Agency on Aging, Northern Idaho
2120 Lakewood Drive, Suite B
Coeur d'Alene, ID 83814
208-667-3179
http://www.aaani.org

Illinois

Little Brothers/Friends of the Elderly
Chicago Chapter
355 N. Ashland Ave.
Chicago, IL 60607-1019
312-455-1000
http://chicago.littlebrothers.org/

Indiana

Indy Links/Charity-Volunteer
http://www.indylinks.com/Society-
    Culture/Organizations/Charity-
    Volunteer/index.html

Real Services
1151 S. Michigan Street
South Bend, IN 46601
574-233-8205
http://www.realservices.org/

Iowa

Iowa Department on Aging
Jessie M. Parker Building
510 E. 12th Street, Suite 2
Des Moines, IA 50319-9025
515-725-3333
http://www.state.ia.us/government/dea/

Volunteer Iowa
Iowa Commission on Volunteer Service
200 E. Grand Ave.
Des Moines, IA 50309
515-242-4799
http://www.volunteeriowa.org/

Kansas

American Red Cross
Midway Kansas Chapter
1900 E. Douglas
Wichita, KS 67214
316-219-4000
http://midwaykansas.redcross.org/

Kentucky

Elderserve
411 East Muhammad Ali Blvd.
Louisville, KY 40202
502-587-8673
http://www.elderserveinc.org/

Senior Care Experts
145 Thierman Lane
Louisville, KY 40207
502-896-2316
http://www.srcareexperts.org/

Senior Services of Northern Kentucky
1032 Madison Avenue
Covington, KY 41011
859-491-0522
http://www.seniorservicesnky.org/

Louisiana
Volunteer Louisiana
620 Florida St., Suite 210
Baton Rouge, LA 70801
225-342-2038
http://www.volunteerlouisiana.gov/

Maine
Eastern Area Agency on Aging
450 Essex St.
Bangor, ME 04401
800-432-7812
http://www.eaaa.org/

Office of Elder Services
Maine Department of Health and Human
    Services
11 State House Station
32 Blossom Lane
Augusta, ME 04333
207-287-9200
http://www.maine.gov/dhhs/oes/

Maryland
Volunteer Maryland
301 W. Preston St. 15th Floor
Baltimore, MD 212101
410-767-6203
http://www.volunteermaryland.org/

Massachusetts
Coastline Elderly Services
1646 Purchase St.
New Bedford, MA 02740
508-999-6400
http://coastlineelderly.org/

Little Brothers/Friends of the Elderly
Boston Chapter
3305 Washington St.
Jamaica Plain, MA 02130-2639
617-524-8882
http://boston.littlebrothers.org/

Michigan
Little Brothers/Friends of the Elderly
Upper Peninsula Michigan Chapter
527 Hancock St.
Hancock, MI 49930-2018
906-482-6944
http://houghton.littlebrothers.org/

Minnesota
Little Brothers/Friends of the Elderly
Minneapolis/St. Paul Chapter
1845 E. Lake St.
Minneapolis, MN 55407-1859
612-721-6215
http://www.littlebrothersmn.org/

Mississippi
Mississippi Commission for Volunteer
    Service
3825 Ridgewood Rd. Suite 601
Jackson, MS 39211
601-432-6779
http://www.mcvs.org/

Mississippi Department of Human Services
750 N. State St.
Jackson, MS 39202
601-359-4500
http://www.mdhs.state.ms.us/

Missouri
Mid-East Area Agency on Aging
14535 Manchester Rd.
Manchester, MO 63011-3960
800-AGE-6060
http://www.mid-eastaaa.org/

Montana
Missoula Aging Services
337 Stephens Ave.
Missoula, MT 59801
406-728-7682
http://www.missoulaagingservices.org/

Nebraska
Little Brothers/Friends of the Elderly
Omaha Chapter
1941 S. 42nd St. Suite 127
Omaha, NE 68105-2942
402-884-6641
http://omaha.littlebrothers.org/

Nevada
Nevada Rural Counties Retired and
    Senior Volunteer Program (RSVP)
2621 Northgate Lane, Suite 6
Carson City, NV 89706
775-687-4680
http://www.nevadaruralrsvp.org/

New Hampshire
LifeWise Community
Volunteer Opportunities
PO Box 2120
Hampton, NH 03843-2120
603-929-0832
http://www.lifewise-nh.org/

Volunteer New Hampshire
http://www.volunteernh.org/html/home.
    htm

New Jersey
The Bright & Beautiful Therapy Dogs
80 Powder Mill Road
Morris Plains, NJ 07950
973-292-3316
http://www.golden-dogs.org/

Daughters of Israel
Cooperman Family Building
1155 Pleasant Valley Way
West Orange, NJ 07052
973-731-5100
http://www.doigc.org

Rebuilding Together—Essex County
PO Box 32171
Newark, NJ 07102
973-642-6100
http://www.rebuildingtogether-newark.
    org/

Volunteer New Jersey
http://www.volunteernewjersey.org/vnj/

New Mexico
Open Hands
2976 Rodeo Park Dr. East
Santa Fe, NM 87505
505-428-2320
http://www.openhands.org/

New York
Catholic Charities of Buffalo
525 Washington Street
Buffalo, NY 14203
71-856-4494
http://www.ccwny.org/

New York State Office for the Aging
2 Empire State Plaza
Albany, NY 12223-1251
800-342-9871
http://www.aging.ny.gov/

NYC Community Service
http://www.ny.com/community/

UJA Foundation of New York
HOPE (Homebound Outreach Project
    Elderly)
http://www.ujafedny.org/volunteer-
    opportunity/view/746-hope--
    homebound-outreach-project-elderly-
    -volunteer

North Carolina
American Red Cross
Central North Carolina Chapter
Volunteer Services
4737 University Dr.
Durham, NC 27717-2509
919-489-4026
http://centralnorthcarolina.redcross.org/

North Dakota
Lutheran Social Services of
    North Dakota
Bismarck: 701-223-1510
Fargo: 701-235-7341
Grand Forks: 701-772-7577
Minot: 701-838-7800
Williston: 701774-0749
http://www.lssnd.org/

Ohio
Gift of Time Ohio
PO Box 866
Grove City, OH 43123
614-875-2100
http://www.giftoftimeohio.com/

Good Bears of the World
PO Box 13097
Toledo, OH 43613
419-531-5365
http://www.goodbearsoftheworld.org/

Little Brothers/Friends of the Elderly
Cincinnati Chapter
5530 Colerain Ave.
Cincinnati, OH 45239-6802
513-542-7555
http://cincinnati.littlebrothers.org/

Oklahoma
United Way of Central Oklahoma
PO Box 837
Oklahoma City, OK 73101
405-523-3581
http://www.unitedwayokc.org/

Oregon
Oregon Volunteer Services
500 Summer St. NE E93
Salem, OR 97301
503-945-8994
http://www.oregonvolunteers.org

Pennsylvania
Little Brothers/Friends of the Elderly
Philadelphia Chapter
642 N. Broad St.
Philadelphia, PA 19130-3409
215-765-8118
http://philadelphia.littlebrothers.org/

Franklin and Marshall College
Elderly Volunteer Opportunities
415 Harrisburg Ave.
Lancaster, PA 17603
717-291-393
http://www.fandm.edu/x19019

Rhode Island
2-1-1 United Way Rhode Island
PO Box 774
Woonsocket, RI 02895
401-766-2300
http://www.211ri.org/

South Carolina
SCANPO: South Carolina Association of
     Nonprofit Organizations
2711 Middleburg Dr., Suite 201
Columbia, SC 29204
803-929-0399
http://www.scanpo.org/

South Dakota
Local Volunteer Opportunities
South Dakota
http://www.hud.gov/local/sd/
     community/volunteeropps.cfm

Senior Meals
James Valley Community Center
300 West First
Mitchell, SD 57301
605-995-8440
http://www.cityofmitchell.org/

Tennessee
Catholic Charities of Tennessee
30 White Bridge Rd.
Nashville, TN 37205
615-352-3087
http://www.cctenn.org/

Texas
The Senior Source
3910 Harry Hines Blvd.
Dallas, TX 75219
214-823-5700
http://www.theseniorsource.org/

Volunteer Center of North Texas
2800 Live Oak St.
Dallas, TX 75204
866-797-8268
http://www.volunteernorthtexas.org/

Utah
Adopt-A-Native-Elder Program
PO Box 3410
Park City, UT 84060
435-649-0535
http://www.anelder.org

Utah Commission on Volunteers
324 South State Street, Suite 500
Salt Lake City, UT 84111
801-538-8700
http://volunteers.utah.gov/

Vermont
Elderly Services, Inc.
112 Exchange St.
Middlebury, VT 05753
802-388-3983
http://www.elderlyservices.org/

Virginia
Virginia Service Volunteer Opportunities
Virginia Department of Social Services
801 E. Main St. 15th Floor
Richmond, VA 23219-2901
800-638-3839
http://www.vaservice.org/

Washington
Volunteer Washington.org
Seattle Works
1625 19th Ave.
Seattle, WA 98122
206-324-0808
http://www.volunteerwashington.org/

Volunteer Connections
201 NE 73rd St., Suite 101
Vancouver, WA 98665
360-735-3683
http://www.1-800-volunteer.org/
1800Vol/human-services-council/
OpenAboutOrganizationAction.
do?organizationId=224142

Washington, DC
National Senior Citizens Law Center
1444 Eye St. NW Suite 1100
Washington, DC 20005
202-289-6976
http://www.nsclc.org/

West Virginia
Volunteer WV
710 Central Ave.
Charleston, WV 25302
304-558-0111
http://www.volunteerwv.org/

Wisconsin
Oneida Tribe of Indians of Wisconsin
Senior Center
134 Riverdale Dr.
Oneida, WI 54155
800-867-1551
http://www.oneidanation.org

West Madison Senior Coalition
517 N. Segoe Road, Suite 309
Madison, WI 53705
608-238-7368
http://www.westmadisonseniorcoalition.
org/

Wyoming
Serve Wyoming
229 E. 2nd St., Suite 203
Casper, WY 82601
866-737-8304
www.servewyoming.org/

Volunteers of America/Montana and
Wyoming
1309 Coffeen Ave, Suite A
Sheridan, WY 82801
307-672-0475
http://www.voawymt.org/

Books

Gay, Kathlyn. *Volunteering: The Ultimate Teen Guide*. Lanham, MD: Scarecrow Press, 2004.

Kelly, Evelyn. *Alzheimer's Disease*. Broomall, PA: Chelsea House Publishers, 2008.

Newell, Patrick. *Volunteering to Help Seniors*. New York: Children's Press, 2000.

Works Consulted

Bass, Sharon L. "Nursing-Home Pets a Boon to Residents." *The New York Times,* http://www.nytimes.com/1986/06/01/nyregion/nursing-home-pets-a-boon-to-residents.html?&pagewanted=1

Kimeldorf, Martin. *The Grandfriends Project*. http://amby.com/kimeldorf/intergenerational/GFP_01.html

Lampman, Lisa B. *Helping a Neighbor in Crisis: How to Encourage When You Don't Know What to Say*. Carol Stream, IL: Tyndale House Publishers, 1999.

Meals on Wheels Association of America, http://www.mowaa.org.

Ryan, Bernard. *Helping the Ill, the Poor and the Elderly*. New York: Ferguson Publishing Co., 1998.

Saint Louis University. "Doggie Robot Eases Loneliness in Nursing Home Residents as Well as Real Dog, Study Finds." *ScienceDaily,* February 26, 2008. http://www.sciencedaily.com/-/releases/2008/02/080225213636.htm.

"Students Make Scrapbooks out of Seniors' Lives," *The Indianapolis Star,* December 21, 2009.

On the Internet

Family Guide to Volunteering
    http://www-tc.pbskids.org/zoom/grownups/action/pdfs/volunteer_guide.pdf

Senior Resources at Don't Almost Give
    http://www.dontalmostgive.org/Volunteer/Seniors.asp

You Can Help Seniors at PBS Kids
    http://pbskids.org/zoom/activities/action/way06.html

Index

Tamra Orr works from her home in the Pacific Northwest.

Tamra Orr is author of more than 250 books for readers of all ages. She believes that helping others who need us is the key to making this world the kind of place where she wants to raise her four children. Her children are helping to do this by being involved in an organization for homeless youth, Search and Rescue, and Habitat for Humanity. Tamra is also involved in the Adopt-a-Platoon organization, writing letters to those fighting overseas.